M000309214

LINES FOR ALL OCCASIONS

Cop-Outs & Alibis

KNOCK KNOCK®
VENICE, CALIFORNIA

Created and published by Knock Knock
1635-B Electric Ave.
Venice, CA 90291
knockknockstuff.com

This book is a work of humor meant solely for
entertainment purposes. Actually utilizing the
lines contained herein may be illegal or lead to
bodily injury. The publisher and anyone associated
with the production of this book do not advocate
breaking the law. In no event will Knock Knock be
liable to any reader for any damages, including
direct, indirect, incidental, special, consequential,
or punitive arising out of or in connection with the
use of the lines contained in this book. So there.

ISBN: 978-160106782-1
UPC: 825703-50119-3

10 9 8 7 6 5 4 3 2 1

Contents

"Sorry, I have this condition where it looks like I'm listening when I'm really not."

Introduction

The truth hurts; in many situations it is best to avoid it entirely. Are you going to tell your brother that you can't come for Christmas because his wife is a grating shrew? Are you going to tell your stylist that she gave you the worst haircut ever? Are you going to tell your boss that the project is late because you stayed up all night rereading *The Stand*?

Because we can't tell the truth
all the time, we need to keep
an arsenal of cop-outs and
alibis at hand so that we can
keep the peace, save our jobs
and our relationships, and
get out of seeing our friend's
daughter attempt Sondheim.
This little book should do
the less-than-truthful trick.

There's always the question of
whether it's ethical to lie, even
if it's harmless. (Not that cop-
outs and alibis are always lies,
per se. Often they're brilliantly
calibrated truths delivered
just so for maximum effect!)
People who study this stuff
agree: lies can help maintain
relationships and make you
feel better about yourself.

Since you can support most claims with some sort of evidence, we'll go with the experts who tell us lying can be good. (There's an alibi right there.) Researchers at the University of Toronto found that the skills you need to be a good liar—quick thinking and the ability to use information to your advantage—are signs of intelligence and predictors of success. Further, lying expert Robert Feldman found that "convincing lying is actually associated with good social skills."

In *Cop-Outs & Alibis for All Occasions*, we give you guidance in a variety of situations to show off your intelligence and those social skills, covering your professional, personal, and public lives. We've got cop-outs for the workplace, your love life, and your relationships with friends and family. We also cover alibis you tell to people when you're out and about, and the special cop-outs you save for yourself. Finally, we cite some of the best lines from the famous and infamous, for those times when you need professional help.

Don't forget to practice your lines to make them more believable, particularly if you plan to deliver one of these gems in person. And of course, you can also cop-out on your cop-outs, and send them via email. According to Feldman, people are far more likely to lie over email than they are face to face.

If you're not much of an actor and you find it hard to pull off sincerity when none is present, these lines will be even better for you. If they don't make you more believable, at least they are funny. Or just plain bizarre. You may not get away with it, but if you crack up your target, or perplex them completely, they may forgive you a lot faster.

George Washington, the very image of honesty, wrote, "It is better to offer no excuse than a bad one." We couldn't agree more. Bad excuses are a scourge upon our land. Use the cop-outs and alibis here and you'll have no excuse to use a bad excuse again.

WORK

WE KNOW THAT YOU'RE DEDICATED
to your job, that you give 100
percent at least 73 percent of the
time. But things happen. You're
late, your project is late, or you
simply dropped the ball. There are
some workplaces where you can tell
the truth: the project bored me, I
was afraid to call that crazy client,
I can't stand working with George.
However, you don't work there.

Tune In; Cop Out

To keep your job, it's best to have a supply of cop-outs and alibis handy. When things go wrong, you can blame technology or other coworkers or you can spout some jargonny nonsense that everyone pretends to understand. If you need to wiggle out of a deadly project, we've got you covered. If you're late or need to skip a day

altogether, we provide reasons
for that, too. Occasionally these
cop-outs will be the truth. You're
destined to actually lose work to
a tech meltdown or get delayed by
insane traffic. Your job is to get
good enough in the telling that
your coworkers don't know
the difference.

Cop-outs and alibis are an essential part of your career toolbox,
as important as your people skills
and technical savvy. If you don't
occasionally get out of a brutal
meeting or take a day off, you'll
likely go nuts, and then you won't
be productive at all. Better to use
a little white lie to keep everyone
happy. We promise—even your
boss is doing this. Especially when
she fires people.

Laziness

I was prepared for this meeting
in a totally unscripted, improv-
comedy sort of way.

———•———

Napping at my desk is an inviolable
aspect of my Spanish siesta culture.

———•———

This is how they do it in the Teamsters.

———•———

I didn't write that proposal, so I
couldn't know we left that out.

———•———

I'm still waiting on a signature
from purchasing.

———•———

I couldn't get enough buy-in, so I thought
I'd bring it up at our next staff meeting.

———•———

The client didn't respond to my
email asking for clarification.

I can't do the team-building
exercise. I'm an introvert.

———•·•———

I couldn't predict there would be a
hurricane on the day I wanted to ship.

———•·•———

I can't make people call me back.

———•·•———

I would've worked on the pitch, but
I thought I was supposed to catch.

———•·•———

I sent it from home, but forgot we
don't have Pages at the office.

———•·•———

I had so much on my plate. You
know, wearing too many hats. I ran
it up the flagpole to see who would
salute, but didn't get a hit on my ping.

———•·•———

Taking ownership of this project
goes against my belief in collective
production for the common good.

I don't have the correct synergy
to envision those outcomes.

———✦———

You're so much better at Power
Point presentations than I am.

———✦———

I'm more of a big-picture person.

Blame Technology

I didn't realize that I had "all-caps" on.

———✦———

I forgot the password. And my
security question. And my
mother's maiden name.

———✦———

I can never figure out Excel.

———✦———

It's just too technical—I'm not
sure you would understand.

———✦———

It got lost in the cloud.

I have to wait for the social media
feedback loop to kick in before I
can work on that any further.

We're in beta testing and
I really can't say when
we might be ready.

I was going to work on that, but
I'm waiting for some feedback
from our developers in India.

Professional Liars

When you need a complicated lie, hire a professional. For a fee, a Minnesota company will lie
for you. They primarily serve job seekers, and
will, according to their website, "assist you in
obtaining the fictitious reference, the little white
lie, or the alibi that you need." Gaps in your
résumé, lack of references, fired from a job?
Paladin Deception Services can provide recom-
mendations and proof of a stronger job history,
among other services. What could go wrong?

The IT team needs to install an
upgrade—it could be a while.

———⋅•⋅———

My GPS sent me out of state.

———⋅•⋅———

There was a huge spider
between me and the door.

———⋅•⋅———

I forgot to unblock you.

———⋅•⋅———

I couldn't understand
your emoticons.

———⋅•⋅———

I was afraid you'd misunderstand the
tone of my email as angry and bitter.

Tardiness

Hackers broke into my alarm clock.

———⋅•⋅———

My doctor insisted
that I get more sleep.

Sorry I was late today. I was up late last night volunteering to raise awareness of how small business owners are the driving force of our economy . . . Boss.

———

I was late delivering that last report because my computer is slow and on my salary I can't afford an upgrade.

———

The ignition switch in my car is under a recall.

———

My therapist is encouraging me to awaken to my own body clock.

———

Since when does a plane ever take off on time?

———

My religion prohibits me from engaging in heavy lifting.

Going Mental

Should you take a mental health day, even if it requires an alibi? Absolutely, say researchers. Doing so can help you avoid a longer break when accumulated stress makes you truly ill down the line. A ComPsychCorp study showed that 82% of Americans take mental health days. Just try to pick a day that's not too busy at work, and call in early. Then be sure to use the day to truly recharge—and don't feel guilty.

I got stuck in a roundabout.

I had a brisket in the oven.

I can't talk to clients anymore because my shrink says I need to cut out codependent relationships.

I forgot that I can't teleport.

Firing Someone

You're so efficient that we've
run out of work for you.

———•◦•———

You're overqualified; you make
everyone else look bad.

———•◦•———

We're holding you
back in your career.

———•◦•———

You're a little too much
of a team player.

———•◦•———

We're making a few cutbacks
in the "you" department.

———•◦•———

The company is doing well, other than
in its ability to pay its employees.

———•◦•———

We just couldn't find space
on the reorganized team.

The merger means there are
certain redundancies.

———••———

It's our job to maximize profits for
our shareholders—so you have to go.

———••———

Think of the bright side—you've
always wanted to learn to paint!

To a Minion

I'd do it myself, but I have
to manage up—and that
takes too much time.

———••———

You know, the go-getters in this
office stay late and help the team out.

———••———

If I paid you minimum wage, how would
we pay all those stock dividends?

———••———

It's just the corporate culture.

We need the private jet because my
time is just so damn valuable.

———•—•———

What can I say—crap rolls downhill.

Inappropriate Behavior

I read somewhere
that "hotness" is an important
quality in hiring an assistant.

———•—•———

If there's one thing I learned
from my time on the field, there's
nothing like a good butt slap
to motivate your secretary.

———•—•———

This isn't pornography;
it's research for an article I'm
writing on pornography.

———•—•———

It couldn't have been me that
xeroxed my ass—I was in the
executive bathroom throwing up.

Playing Hooky

Two words: bad clams.

I was dangerously deficient
in Vitamin D; the doctor
prescribed an immediate
sunshine infusion.

I was working on
my masterpiece.

I thought I won the lottery.
I was wrong.

Office Etiquette

Your lunch bag looks
kind of like mine.

I was going to come back and
wash my mugs later.

I was going to fill up
the pot, but you're so
much better at making
coffee than I am.

It's hard to tell which bin
is for recyclables.

The water bottle is too heavy
for me to switch out.

Giant Clown, Again?

The train from Cardiff to London delayed by a
giant clown on the tracks? That's just one of the
excuses offered in Britain for late trains. Other
gems explaining service disruptions: signalman
trapped in toilet, driver attacked by seagull,
and dew on the tracks. The absurdity of the
excuses has inspired a Twitter parody—TLF
Travel Alerts—that posts excuses for delays
and closures such as minotaurs, angry rat kings,
and Earth Wizard and Fire Elf battles.

ROMANCE

When all you need isn't love

HONESTY IS THE MOST IMPORTANT thing in a romantic relationship. Actually, that's a lie. Probably the most important things are the little half-truths that spare your partner's feelings or cover your butt. From the first "meet cute" or "meet creepy," you need a backup plan. Perhaps you need to deflect someone because you're just not into him and you want to let him down easy. Perhaps you simply forgot

(S)he Asked for It

As Aaron Ben-Zeév, Ph.D., writes in *Psychology Today*, humans get elaborate when rationalizing affairs. We pose as altruists ("Without the affair, I would have left my spouse") or diminish our guilt ("It's not my fault; it's hormones") or feelings ("It's just sex"). But cheaters, take heed; the author warns: "When you have a very good justification, one reason is usually enough; when there is no such justification, one needs to accumulate sufficient excuses as no one of them is likely to be convincing."

a date or an anniversary or your marriage vows. Perhaps you're not in the mood for any slap and tickle or you want a kind way out of a relationship that should have ended before it began.

If you're going to test run a cop-out with a relative stranger, you don't have to be particularly good at it or even particularly believable. Have some fun with it. Later she will remember you not as the insulting jerk but the *amusing* insulting jerk. When using an alibi in a close relationship you've got to be better at it. Your loved one knows all of your tricks. Look for safe places to direct the blame: to yourself, your mother, the government, or strangers. If possible, make it look like you did whatever you did to make your sweetie's life better.

If you feel guilty lying to the one you love, just tell yourself that you're being creative—you're spinning a good yarn. And it does serve the relationship, after all. (You can get extra points for deceiving others while simultaneously deceiving yourself.)

Cheating Hearts & Other Parts

It wasn't a kiss—that's just
how the Inuit say hello.

———•—•———

I was just teaching him how
to properly tune a flute.

———•—•———

Sure, I was looking at her, but
I was thinking about you.

———•—•———

You know how they
spray you with perfume
at Bloomingdale's.

———•—•———

Monogamy is so bourgeois.

———•—•———

I didn't know we weren't
seeing other people.

———•—•———

Yes, it was a French kiss . . . because
he happens to be French.

The heart wants what it wants.
And so, apparently, does my vagina.

⎯⎯·•·⎯⎯

I was just trying to read
the logo on her jeans.

⎯⎯·•·⎯⎯

We were discussing my previously
unexpressed passion for dentistry, one
thing led to another, and suddenly
I'm inspecting her fillings.

⎯⎯·•·⎯⎯

Open relationships
are totally in.

⎯⎯·•·⎯⎯

She came on to me and I didn't
want her feelings to get hurt.

⎯⎯·•·⎯⎯

I went into that store to buy
you something sexy.

⎯⎯·•·⎯⎯

I needed to learn more about
OkCupid for a story I'm writing.

31

She was so drunk, I just wanted to
make sure she got to bed safely.

———•—•———

My phone was dead and I had a
flat, so I went into the strip club
to use the phone to call AAA.

———•—•———

I thought we agreed out-of-town
conferences were fair game.

———•—•———

Shameless flirting is completely
acceptable behavior in Italy.

———•—•———

I meant to be "monogamous," but I
got it mixed up with "magnanimous."

Generally Bad Behavior

If I compliment you too often
you'll get a big head.

———•—•———

I'm not the marrying kind.

I was preparing for a role;
it was method acting.

⸻

I'd get a vasectomy, but I
hear it really hurts.

⸻

I just came out of a bad
relationship—I can only
commit to booty calls.

It's All Latin to Me

Of Latin origin, the word "alibi" means
"in or at another place." It was first used
in the English language in legal contexts,
to describe a plea that one was elsewhere
when a crime was committed. It's worth
noting that you usually can't introduce an
alibi in the middle of a trial. In the US, while
lawyers may keep their defense secret, most
states require early disclosure of alibis so
prosecutors can check their validity.

It's not that I wasn't paying attention to what you were saying, it's that I was just so distracted by your beauty.

I didn't say "I love you" because words cheapen what I feel for you.

Eschewing Responsibility

If I don't go drinking with the guys I'll get left out of deals.

Valentine's Day is such a sexist patriarchal holiday I thought you'd appreciate staying in and watching TV as a form of protest.

My job is so stressful I just don't have the bandwidth to talk about feelings after work.

This engagement ring doesn't have
diamonds since I know how you feel
about indigenous culture exploitation.

――――•―•――――

I'd love to go to your second
cousin's wedding, but you know how
important that golf tournament
is for client development.

Dumping a Date

The voices in my head say no.

――――•―•――――

I'm thinking about questioning
my sexual orientation.

――――•―•――――

I took a vow of celibacy.

――――•―•――――

I really don't want to
ruin our friendship.

――――•―•――――

We're not astrologically compatible.

Hide in Plain Sight

Turn a potentially Orwellian invasion of your privacy into a cheater's BFF. Sign into a location app such as Find My Friends, put your phone on silent, and give it to a pal heading someplace innocent—say, the library. When you get asked, "Where were you last night?" just reply, "I was studying—didn't you see it on Find My Friends?" Boom. Built-in alibi. That is, until the person you're avoiding uses it to show up where you "are."

Let's face it. We're just not that into each other.

———•❖•———

I'm a lousy judge of character.

———•❖•———

I left my wallet in the same car that I previously mentioned was just inexplicably stolen.

———•❖•———

You're nice—too nice.

Forgot Anniversary

Tiffany's was closed.

I left your present at the office.

I remember the day we fell in love,
rather than the day we got married.

It got stuck in customs,
but it's on its way!

I celebrate our marriage every day.

Not Moving In

I don't want you to get too
dependent on me.

Your art will clash with mine.

Your dog and I don't get along.

My horoscope advises against it.

———•◦•———

I need a lot of "me" time.

———•◦•———

I have restless leg syndrome—you'd be
more comfortable in your own bed.

———•◦•———

I need room to create!

Falling Asleep in an Untimely Manner

You just make me feel so
safe and relaxed.

———•◦•———

I thought we were done.

———•◦•———

The kids are just so exhausting.

———•◦•———

I'm still tired from the last time.

———•◦•———

It was the wine.

Not in the Mood

My hamstrings are too tight.

I've got that "not so fresh" feeling.

I talked to my mother tonight.

I've got the *Sesame Street* theme
song stuck in my head.

I just got my euphemism.

I think I'm coming down with something
and I don't want you to catch it.

Breakups

I'll just end up hurting you.

I don't want to ruin you for other people.

When you said you wanted to hear the
"L-word," I thought you meant "leave."

———•———

I'm saving you the trouble
of dumping me.

———•———

I'm electing to resign from this
relationship in order to spend
more time with my dog.

———•———

We just don't have the same
taste in three-way partners:
I like them, you don't.

———•———

My therapist says I need to be
on my own for a while.

———•———

It's because my parents didn't
say they loved me.

———•———

We can never be together because
our names don't hyphenate well.

Look at it this way—now you get
to keep the half of the stuff you
actually cared about anyway.

———•◆•———

It's not you; it's your cat.

———•◆•———

It's not you; it's my penis.

———•◆•———

My shrink says your "me time" involves
way too much of my "me time."

Luv U, Just Nt in Luv w U

If the tables are turned, and you've been told
"I love you—I'm just not *in* love with you," or
another relationship-ender, take inspiration from
Allison Wade. After getting dumped in that most
modern of ways—via text—she began turning
parting words into art. Understandably, the exes
who sent texts like "if i ever see you i will want to
kiss you. but i am, at the moment, quite emotion-
ally unavailable. i have to go to dinner." didn't
show up to Wade's gallery opening.

FAMILY & FRIENDS

When you can't go home again

WE GET A HEAD START INVENTING
cop-outs and alibis to tell our
friends and family. According
to lying expert Victoria Talwar,
children start when they are two
or three, especially those who are
exceptionally bright. And where
do the little minxes get it? They
get it from their parents, of course.
Parents show by example and often
encourage their children toward

That Hungry Dog

No matter how clichéd, kids still offer absurd excuses for missing homework, according to teacher surveys. Some of the best: "My family got a new paper shredder and we had to see if it was working"; "I put it on the TV and the TV blew up"; and a tale about aliens taking it as a sample of human education. Even though today's excuses more often involve wonky computers, "My dog ate it" is still a perennial favorite.

half-truths to save someone's feelings. If you need a cop-out for your tendency to fall back on cop-outs, deflect blame to your parents.

With our families, we need to keep an air of mystery around our lives and we need boundaries. Our parents don't really want to know everything that we're doing and we certainly don't want to know everything that they're doing. No sane human being can attend every single family event, so maintaining a quiver of alibis to get out of one or another is a necessity. If you can't get out of it, a reason that you never showed up is just as essential. (Would you rather ask for permission, or forgiveness? Reasons for both are here.) Similarly, with our friends, we should enjoy their company, but we need to have an out for those times we're a little sick of them, or perhaps our own behavior leaves a little something to be desired.

Rest assured, your friends and family will appreciate your skills as a storyteller. You owe it to the people you love to go the extra mile in crafting the perfect excuse.

Child to Parent

If I clean my room now, I'm just going to have to clean it again in a few months.

———•———

I thought my phone was in my pocket, but I left it in my locker.

———•———

This is not a tantrum; it's a reaction to your cruel failure to spoil me.

———•———

I will eat my vegetables only when all the children of the world get the broccoli they deserve.

———•———

My homework is to practice civil disobedience.

———•———

If I don't sneak out of the house, how will I learn about independence?

———•———

We're just friends.

Is that what that is? I've
never even tried it.

———•—•———

It's just a different time now.
Everybody's doing it.

———•—•———

It's not mine.

Parent to Child

Your dad and I were just
having a discussion.

———•—•———

I did it once—but I regretted
it immediately.

———•—•———

Without my failings you
kids wouldn't have anything
to blame your own on.

———•—•———

I was not a deadbeat dad—I was
practicing "non-invasive" parenting.

You would have resented any tiger-
momming I might have done.

———•◆•———

Just be glad you didn't have my parents.

———•◆•———

I wanted to help you improve
your problem-solving skills.

———•◆•———

Because we didn't know
any better back then.

———•◆•———

Because I said so, that's why.

———•◆•———

It's not mine.

Avoiding Chores

The vacuum cleaner was
all the way upstairs.

———•◆•———

I've got a sensitivity to all
those cleaning products.

I'm training the dog to take itself out.

———◆———

I wasn't sure you were ready
for me to clean that.

———◆———

I know you have your own special
way of putting my clothes away.

———◆———

I didn't wash the dishes because
we're conserving water.

Lost in Translation?

Targeting a scapegoat is a useful, if regret-
table, mode of cop-out. This oddly evocative
term was actually created in a translation
error. In the Bible, God tells Aaron to offer a
sacrificial goat for Yahweh, and one for Azazel
(a demon) to be sent off into the wild, sym-
bolically carrying away the sins of the people.
When William Tyndale translated the Bible in
1530, he mistranslated this "goat for Azazel" as
"the goat that departs" or the "escape goat."

Give it enough time and the garbage will just decompose into nothing sitting right where it is.

———•———

Don't look at it as an "uncut lawn"—it's a "drought-tolerant native plant grassland preserve."

———•———

When you told me "you have to do it" I thought you meant the royal you.

Excusing Non-Attendance

I couldn't stop binge watching *Gilligan's Island*.

———•———

I would've made it to the party, but my team was in the playoffs!

———•———

My iCal got deleted during the iOS upgrade.

No, I really love experimental mime
theater, but my car broke down.

———•◆•———

I just couldn't get the time off
work to make it to great-uncle
Howard's retirement party.

———•◆•———

I was drunk when I
promised to come.

———•◆•———

I was literally tied up.

———•◆•———

I forgot.

Getting Out of Invites

It's my bowling night.

———•◆•———

I'm allergic to your cat.

———•◆•———

Oh, the party is that Saturday?
I'm having my tires rotated.

You Wouldn't Understand

Want an all-purpose way to express your unique point of view without having to explain yourself? Try "It's a ___ thing; you wouldn't understand." At one time, it was a statement about race consciousness ("It's a Black thing; you wouldn't understand"), but it soon became ubiquitous. Now people throw in any old word—"blonde," "New York," "flibbertigibbet," "entitled jerk"— and the argument is over.

I have to go to her family's house for the holiday.

———

My dog doesn't look so good.

———

I'd love to see your daughter's holiday concert, but I already made plans to see another children's musical show tonight.

———

I just got Netflix.

52

I know I said I'd come, but who
holds a wedding on the same day
as the Pro Bowler Association
World Championship?!

———•·•———

My meds aren't strong enough.

———•·•———

Your meds aren't strong enough.

Unvitations

Turns out the invitation didn't
actually say "and guest."

———•·•———

Apparently it's only
immediate family.

———•·•———

It's a really small
wedding, Grandma.

———•·•———

I figured you wouldn't want to
come if your ex was coming.

Explaining the Family

We're WASPs—we don't do family stuff.

I come from a long line of non-huggers. Don't take it personally.

Before we go in, I want you to know that I disagree with everything my family stands for.

It's not that my mother doesn't like you; she just doesn't like new people.

My brother isn't dysfunctional. He's just sensitive.

General Bad Manners

I'm sure she'll get over it in a few days.

My house is too small to host.

Since you're against materialism, I
thought you'd prefer not to get
a Christmas gift this year.

———•·•———

You know me—I never
send thank-you cards.

———•·•———

I'm not avoiding your calls;
I've just decided to take a
hiatus from technology.

———•·•———

Words couldn't express
my gratitude.

———•·•———

I left my wallet in my other pants.

———•·•———

I left my wallet in my other purse.

———•·•———

I thought there were already too
many people helping clean up—I
didn't want to be in the way.

I can't afford stamps.

I baked a cake for you, but on my way
here I gave it to a homeless family.

Roommates

It looked just like the
cleaning toothbrush.

I was under the impression
we shared everything here,
including boyfriends.

I was so smashed I guess I
thought it was the bathroom.

It's not my music that's too loud,
it's the walls that are too thin.

I ate what was in the fridge because
I wanted to help you on your diet.

Awkward Moments

I thought you guys broke up!

———•————

I just assumed you had been
invited to the party too.

———•————

I told you that a long time ago!

———•————

You're my best friend—and so is she.

You Look Great!

Go ahead. Say it. And know you're keeping the
very fabric of society together. A study published in *Proceedings of the Royal Society B*
found "prosocial," or white lies create closer
ties within a social network versus "antisocial"
lying for personal gain, which damages relationships. "The balance between prosocial and
antisocial lies may set constraints on the struc-
ture of social networks, and hence the shape of
society as a whole," researchers wrote.

IN DENIAL

When you can't tell the truth, even to yourself

WHAT WOULD WE DO WITHOUT
our beloved vices and foibles?
They're what make us human
and interesting. You spend your
life trying to overcome them, but
you'll never be fully successful—
we're all imperfect. Sometimes,
it is healthy to accept your faults
and move on, and sometimes it
is healthy to vocally deny them.
That's where this chapter comes in.

Just Say No

Introverts are great at inventing excuses to avoid social situations, but the experts say you should actually simply say "No." Give it to them straight—"I'm an introvert, I don't like large groups, I don't like parties, I've been out too many times this week, I'm happy at home with Netflix and Fig Newtons." If they keep nudging you to join them after you've been honest, then you have every right to claim that you have a communicable disease.

After a lifetime of self-deception, it is helpful to get a fresh infusion of cop-outs and alibis to tell yourself. You can't be expected to do all of the work, all of the time.

Every part of our lives includes a little self-deception, but there are some areas where we need all the help we can get. This is especially true when it comes to keeping ourselves healthy by eating right and exercising—or not; our careers—or lack thereof; and the way we care for the earth—or don't.

There is evidence that lying to yourself can be a useful trait, especially if it helps overcome obstacles that would seem insurmountable if you thought honestly about them. Self-deception helps us take risks. Ian Leslie, author of *Born Liars*, notes that people who lie to themselves often do better in business— it takes self-deception and excess confidence to pursue grandiose plans when the odds are against success.

Of course, telling yourself that self-deception is the secret to success may just be another personal cop-out. But don't worry, we won't tell anyone.

Political Correctness

I was going to vote, but then I realized that I don't live in a swing state and I still have laundry to do.

All my steak was very happy before it was killed.

I volunteer every Thanksgiving.

I'll just have to wait to be more fuel efficient until after the kids are grown and I don't obviously need this minivan.

I'd recycle if I knew what the numbers meant.

Biking to work? Where would I shower?

I'd walk, but I look so good in my car.

Have you seen how much
pollution there is in China?!

I didn't forget the paper towels,
I just think we should start
being mindful of our waste and
start using reusable towels.

Ingesting Substances

This pack doesn't count because
I bought it before I quit.

Apparently cigarettes help
improve cognition.

I'll switch to menthols
first—they're disgusting.

This marijuana is medicinal.

It's a sin to leave a bottle half-full.

Drug dealers are small
business owners, too, and
they need our support.

———•———

That glass was a lot bigger than
I had originally thought.

———•———

Vodka is Atkins-safe.

———•———

I don't drink *French* amounts of wine.

———•———

Don't ask me how many I had . . .
you know I'm terrible at math.

———•———

In the old days, alcohol was
considered medicine.

———•———

I'm so boring when I'm sober.

———•———

I'm buying all this wine to entertain
with. For a very large dinner party.

Other Vices

My tips are the only thing keeping those Hooters girls off welfare.

The local service economy depends on my spending.

I'm only into porn for the hilarious punny titles.

Delay Your Way to Failure

Take copping-out to the extreme with a practice psychologists call "self-handicapping." Skip studying for an exam, put in a lousy effort on a project, or impede your performance with distractions. When you fail, you'll be able to blame it on these negative strategies rather than your abilities. And if you do well in spite of them—bonus! Note: this practice may be harmful in the long run to your success and self-esteem.

The way I see it, a 250-million-
to-one chance at winning the
lottery is still a chance.

—•—

I still plan on turning this experience
into an object lesson of what not to do.

Weight

I just haven't grown out of my baby fat.

—•—

I just haven't found my guru yet.

—•—

Weight Watchers has too much math.

—•—

I'm just big boned.

—•—

What you see here is just a setup for an
unbelievably dramatic "after" photo.

—•—

Tomorrow's not just another
day—it's *the* day.

I'd have to buy new clothes
if I lost weight.

———•·•———

Well, at least I'm not obese.

Food

If we weren't supposed to
eat meat, it wouldn't
taste so darned good.

———•·•———

I need meat to sustain my
substantial muscle mass.

———•·•———

Potatoes are a plant, so
technically a vegetable. So
French fries count.

———•·•———

My dream diet's still out
there somewhere.

———•·•———

The problem with good nutrition
is that it tastes nutritious.

No Time Like Tomorrow

Yes, your sock drawer is in disarray and that article on the philosophical underpinnings of *The Simpsons* is still unread, but you shouldn't need such ploys to procrastinate on other tasks. In a *New York Times* article titled "How to Stop Time," writer Anna Della Subin asks, "Why not view procrastination not as a defect, an illness or a sin, but as an act of resistance against the strictures of time and productivity imposed by higher powers?" Rise up!—to your couch.

You'll see, soon science will tell us to eat a lot more fat and carbs.

I just don't like the texture of tofu.

Isn't wine one of the main components of the Mediterranean diet?

Fitness

My workouts are more efficient,
so they can be shorter.

———•◦•———

I'll stretch when I get home.

———•◦•———

I'm allergic to sweat.

———•◦•———

5Ks aren't enough of a workout for me.

———•◦•———

I can't say "Namaste" with
a straight face.

———•◦•———

If God had wanted me to run, he
wouldn't have given me boobs this big.

———•◦•———

I'm still recovering from a
traumatic Zumba incident.

———•◦•———

It said not to start without a doctor's okay.

I decided to stay home from the gym
and concentrate on my protein intake.

I just get so bored at the gym.

I'll go back to the gym
as soon as I find the right
pair of sneakers.

My gym membership ran
out, and the renewal
costs too much.

I haven't found a good-enough
gym since I moved.

No one has ever showed me
how to use those machines.

There's so much conflicting
workout information, I just
don't know where to begin.

I just need a little warm-up.

It's been proven that
growing abs need a good
long resting period.

Chores

I'll fix that leaky faucet
tomorrow for sure.

I'd rather wait to do
the laundry so my clothes
develop that nice aristocratic
patina to them.

I'm not taking out
the trash because
I'm trying to compost.

Why make the bed if it's
just going to be slept
in again anyway?

Hygiene

Have you seen the price
of toothpaste lately?

I've developed a soap allergy.

The shampoo was not cruelty-free.

I am cultivating good bacteria.

If things don't get dirty, how can
one really appreciate clean?

My body odor is part of a self-
esteem research project.

Career

Success is afraid of me.

I don't want to overshadow my family.

Getting a job would be
giving in to The Man.

———•◆•———

Hey, I may not be fulfilled,
but at least it pays the bills.

———•◆•———

My grandmother came to
me in a dream to warn me
away from law school.

Stopped for Z.U.I.

If you're caught driving under the influence in
New Jersey, try to convince the cop that your
car is a Zamboni. When an NJ man was cited
for drunk driving a Zamboni in 2005, a judge
overturned the charges. Since a Zamboni can't
drive on highways or carry passengers, they
aren't considered motor vehicles. But don't try
it in Minnesota. A tipsy Zamboni driver in Apple
Valley, MN, pled guilty to gross misdemeanor
D.W.I. in 2012 and got two years probation.

In this economy, I'm just lucky
to have a full-time job.

———————

I'll ask for that raise the
next time my boss is in a
good mood and Mercury
isn't in retrograde.

———————

I'm going to start my book as
soon as the research is finished.

———————

I would've received that promotion,
but that #&*$ is such a suck-up.

Personal Finance

It's okay to take the money
out of my savings account—
this suit is an investment in
my future employment.

———————

I made that money at night, so
technically it's not taxable.

It's not a Ponzi scheme. I'm
a "brand ambassador."

———•◦•———

Well, I brought my lunch every
other day this week . . .

Love

What? You think I should just settle?

———•◦•———

I'm too busy right now to date.

———•◦•———

Once I get my finances squared away,
then I'll think about settling down.

———•◦•———

I just haven't met "Ms. Right."

———•◦•———

Why rush into a relationship? 50%
of marriages end in divorce anyway.

———•◦•———

It's hard to find someone who
appreciates all of my idiosyncrasies.

OUT & ABOUT

When you need to explain yourself to others

STEP OUT OF YOUR HOME AND
you're liable to find yourself doing
something wrong. The world
is one big minefield of opportunities to embarrass yourself.
Without a doubt, as soon as you
arrive somewhere you shouldn't
be, you'll run into your mom's
best friend. (Why she's in the sex
shop too is not your problem;
you need to think of yourself.)

Would You Believe...?

If you want to avoid jury duty, keep your wits about you. One Los Angeles pet owner explained that she couldn't serve because "The mutt upstairs would break in" and her dog would get knocked up. The lame excuse became a favorite story for L.A.'s jury assignment supervisor. In Denver, a woman called a radio show to boast that she'd avoided duty by feigning insanity. Unfortunately, the judge she'd fooled was listening—and had her arrested.

You may be good at handling the demands and expectations of your workplace, your loved ones, and yourself, but that is just scratching the surface. You've got to deal with teachers, police officers, and total strangers. Now you need yet another supply of cop-outs and alibis. Sure, you can reuse lines from earlier chapters on the strangers in your world; some are all-purpose. However, you'll need some stranger-specific ones as well.

Being out in the world gives you opportunities to practice some of the lines herein, since you can reuse them with different people. In many cases, you can also use them without worrying about whether the person believes you or not. He or she is a stranger, after all. Odds are, they'll believe you anyway. According to expert Robert Feldman, "a lot of the time, we don't want to detect lies in other people. We are unwilling to put forward the cognitive effort to suspect the veracity of statements, and we aren't motivated to question people when they tell us things we want to hear." As long as you've maintained your dignity, it's all that really matters.

In Trouble with the Law

Oh, so that's the speedometer!

I was showing my kids what
crappy driving looks like.

I don't have a driver's license because
I am a citizen of the world.

My gas pedal was stuck—it's being
recalled by the manufacturer.

I guess at a certain point, even non-
alcoholic beer will get you drunk.

It depends on what your
definition of "stop" is, officer.

I leave the blinker on because, hey,
you never know when you'll need
to take a last-minute left turn.

Why else do you think they
call them bumpers?

———

That gas pedal looks an
awful lot like the brake.

———

Why yes, officer, I do
carry all my jewels and
silverware around at night
in a large, black sack.

———

Officer, I was just asking for
directions, but she seemed really
nice and we just hit it off.

In a Sex Shop

I'm doing research for my novel.

———

I thought the sign said "sax" shop.

———

I'm looking for a gag gift.

In a Strip Club

They have the best fries here.

I just come for the conversation
and camaraderie.

These girls really just
want to talk to someone,
and I can provide that.

In the Café

My friend Godot will be
here any minute now.

I bought a muffin and
coffee—that entitles me
to sit here all day.

I need extra room for
my big personality.

In School

I didn't plagiarize.
It's "found art."

I thought this was an oral
homework assignment.

I can't write anything longer
than 140 characters.

"Officer, I Can Explain…"

Children are known for lying, but we have to salute the ambition of one young Norwegian boy. Early one winter morning, this adventurous ten-year-old stole his parents' car, then with his baby sister in tow, started off towards his grandparents' house, about 38 miles away. When he drove off the road and ended up in a ditch, he claimed to be a dwarf who had forgotten his driver's license. This kid either has a future in theater—or in politics.

I was too busy trying to memorize the
world capitals. Ask me Burkina Faso!

My dog ate my router.

I don't trust spellcheck.

My professor gets off on failing me.

Plagiarism? I prefer to call my book
report the sincerest form of flattery.

College has always been about
the "Three R's": Rest, Relaxation,
and getting Really baked.

Hackers stole all my
sexting pics, so I had to delete
everything in the cloud.

I was texting the principal to tell her
what a brilliant rhetorician you are.

In the Doctor's Office

I *had* an apple a day.

My herbalist says I'm fine.

I weigh a lot less than that—
I had a big breakfast.

At the Gym

It's a recovery day, so I'm
doing a lighter workout.

I don't want to bulk up, so I only
do light weights and lots of reps.

My lower back issues
prevent me from doing a lot of
these machines and classes.

I've had the flu, so I'm just
easing back into it.

No Accounting for Taste

After repeatedly violating Idaho nudity laws, the owner of Boise's Erotic City strip club handed out sketchpads to patrons and called it "art night." The police saw things differently, citing three dancers for breaking the law—which only protects full nudity with "serious artistic merit." Said a police spokeswoman, "It was pretty obviously they were attempting to use artistic expression to get around the law." Sadly for the owner, the police didn't give extra credit for creativity.

In the Store

I figured you could always use
the practice folding clothes.

That was a line? I thought you
were waiting for the restroom.

I would've hung up all those things
I tried on, but I'm in such a hurry.

Sorry to hold up the line,
but I'm doing my civic duty
by putting all these pennies
back into circulation.

——•◦•——

The tomatoes at the
bottom of that stack looked
so much fresher.

To the Needy

I don't have any small bills.

——•◦•——

I donate to the Red Cross.

——•◦•——

My wife makes all the donations.

——•◦•——

I pay for everything in Bitcoin.

——•◦•——

I put all my cash into gold so
it's safe during the impending
zombie apocalypse.

Badly Behaving Pets

I don't know what got into
him—he never does that.

If I cut the grass, how will all the
mice hide from the birds?

But he never barks when I'm home.

Cats can't be decimating the
bird population—mine has
only ever killed five or six.

I took him to that free
six-week training class.

He hates it when he
has to be on a leash.

She loves people so much she just
wants to lick them all over.

I would pick up after my dog,
but I'd rather not contribute
to plastic bag waste.

I just used my last poop bag.

I'd pick up the dog poop, but
he's just going to make more.

Being a Not-So-Great Neighbor

I'm going to trim that
bush back as soon as my friend
returns my electric trimmer.

Paint is so toxic, I've decided it's better
the house have that weathered look.

I'm in between lawn services right now.

I think leaves should just
degrade naturally.

I'm sure the sun will melt that ice
before I can find the salt in my garage.

———•◦•———

If I take down that old rotting tree,
where will all the chipmunks live?

Religion

The word "pew" makes me giggle.

———•◦•———

Sunday brunch is JUST like church.

———•◦•———

What Would Jesus Do? He'd forgive me.

———•◦•———

I'd burst into flames if I
walked into a church.

———•◦•———

I believe the Buddhist thing to do
here is to just shrug and walk away.

———•◦•———

You can chalk that indiscretion
up to karma.

Being the Landlord

In a building with this much vintage charm, leaks just come with the territory.

———◆———

Who needs heat when we've got global warming?

———◆———

Calling an exterminator violates the tenets of my PETA membership.

It's Chicken!

You gotta give Burger King credit for cojones. When its 2005 marketing campaign for Chicken Fries—featuring fake metal band "Coq Roq"—drew backlash, BK doubled down with absurd excuses. Besides offending some with the band's name, the campaign drew fire when the Coq Roq website posted Polaroid-like shots of young women captioned, "Groupies love the Coq." An executive blamed the captioning on technical malfunctions in the programming.

With rent this cheap, you
get what you pay for.

———•———

Those repairs will be made just as
soon as the HOA approves them.

When You're Lost

I didn't know whether you
meant your left or mine.

———•———

I'm not going to ask
for directions . . . what if
that guy's wrong?

———•———

Who could possibly figure
out this map interface?

———•———

How could I pay attention to
you when I'm trying to drive?

———•———

This GPS just isn't working right at all.

Being Rude

Sorry, I have this condition
where it looks like I'm listening
when I'm really not.

———•—•———

Lethargy is a defense mechanism to
mask my complete indifference.

———•—•———

My patience is limited only by time.

In Politics

It's all-too-easy to call it a bribe, until
you're the one on the receiving end.

———•—•———

I prefer the Latin term for "getting
things done": quid pro quo.

———•—•———

Don't blame me, I voted
for the welfare state.

WELL-KNOWN
WAFFLING

When the famous start backpedaling

IF A RUN-OF-THE-MILL COP-OUT
or alibi isn't quite up to the situation, it may be time to turn to
the professionals. Why reinvent
the wheel when there are famous
people—politicians, entertainers,
reality TV stars—who come up
with brilliant and egregious cop-
out and alibis every day? Whether
part of a script or song, or a
whopper that slips out at a press

You're . . . Safe!

Don't count on Larry David getting you sprung, but one very lucky guy hit that jackpot. Juan Catalan was in jail for five and a half months on murder charges before footage from David's HBO show *Curb Your Enthusiasm* helped free him. Turns out a scene that landed on the cutting-room floor showed Catalan at a Los Angeles Dodgers game at the time of the murder he allegedly committed. Almost sounds like a *Seinfeld* bit.

conference, there are greater minds than ours perfecting the art.

We have no evidence that famous people play with the truth more than anyone else. They just do it far more publicly than we do. Further, as everything in their lives is so minutely scrutinized, they are less likely to get away with a juicy cop-out. You can feel sorry for them or pretend to rise above the resulting gossip, or you can capitalize on the situation and stash the alibi away for use in the future.

Using famous cop-outs and alibis does carry some risk. It's possible that the person on whom you try it out will recognize the line. If this happens, just smile like that was your intention all along. There is a good chance that he'll be impressed with your wide cultural knowledge and memory and you can have a good laugh over it. If he thinks you're a pretentious poser, it's no loss: use another one of the cop-outs to get out of the conversation, and go find another patsy.

Celebrities

"In many ways we are closer than we have ever been . . . We have always conducted our relationship privately, and we hope that as we consciously uncouple and coparent, we will be able to continue in the same manner." —Gwyneth Paltrow and Chris Martin on their split

---

"I have severe acid reflux. It started acting up and I could not speak or talk . . . My voice was not strong enough to hold up the song alone." —Ashlee Simpson regarding her lip synching on *Saturday Night Live*

"I've always been very, very naïve." —Paula Deen, during her racial slur scandal

---

"The only thing I'm addicted to is winning." —Charlie Sheen on why Alcoholics Anonymous is for sissies

"I have no clue [why people say I'm insane]. Every time I've heard it, it came from an ugly person's mouth, so I don't care." —Amanda Bynes

---

"I was told that I had my license. My lawyer told me the license is suspended for 30 days, no driving. Then 90 days, then after that you could drive to and from work." —Paris Hilton on why she drove with a suspended license and ended up in jail as a result

---

"I had too much work going on. I had a surgery for my wisdom teeth that went really badly. I had been in the hospital. I had two surgeries on my wisdom teeth. I had four taken out and they had gotten it really badly wrong. They had to drill into my jaw and I was just in really excruciating pain." —Actress Mischa Barton discussing what led to her 5150 hospitalization in 2010

"The heart wants what it wants. There's no logic to those things. You meet someone and you fall in love and that's that."
—Woody Allen on his relationship with his son's sister Soon-Yi

---

"Two months prior to that, I broke my arm in two places, and the doctor, a sort of quack doctor, was giving me a lot of stuff and I was taking it at first to get through the pain. And then there was this weird point when you don't know if you are in pain but you're taking it." —Winona Ryder on the state of "confusion" that led to her shoplifting arrest in 2001

"I was exhausted. It was right off the air. My daughter had a softball game I desperately wanted to go to and I was a little impatient . . . I said some things I shouldn't have said." —ex-CNN host Rick Sanchez on disparaging remarks that got him fired

"I'd sit on my dad's lap and I drive. We're country." —Britney Spears on why she drove with her infant son, Sean, in her lap in 2005

Athletes

"When he said it was flaxseed oil, I just said, 'Whatever.'" —Barry Bonds in grand jury testimony in 2003, regarding "unbeknownst" steroid use

The Othello Error

We think we know when someone is lying, but our own emotions can cloud our judgment. Just ask Othello. Shakespeare's protagonist accuses Desdemona of adultery, which upsets her; he assumes she's lying and kills her. Psychologist Paul Ekman calls this the "Othello error": an honest person who has been accused of lying may be so upset, he or she will actually appear to be lying. Pay attention to cues, but don't let them lead you to disaster.

"I'm sorry you can't dream big and I'm sorry you don't believe in miracles." —Lance Armstrong, addressing skeptics during his 2005 Tour de France victory speech

---

"He beat me because my jockstrap was too tight and because when he serves he farts, and that made me lose my concentration, for which I am famous throughout Zambia." —Tennis player Lighton Ndefwayl on losing a match in 1992

"It was beyond all doubt that the incident was a product of a deliberate act perpetrated by adulterated foodstuff as [the players] could not get up all of a sudden just before the match." —North Korea's football association on why the North Korean soccer team lost a 2009 World Cup qualifying match to South Korea

Film

"I tried to think of the most harmless thing. Something I loved from my childhood. Something that could never ever possibly destroy us. Mr. Stay Puft!" —Dan Aykroyd as Dr. Raymond Stantz in *Ghostbusters*

"But you can't hold a whole fraternity responsible for the behavior of a few sick, perverted individuals. For if you do, then shouldn't we blame the whole fraternity system? And if the whole fraternity system is guilty, then isn't this an indictment of our educational institutions in general? I put it to you, Greg—isn't this an indictment of our entire American society? Well, you can do what you want to us, but we're not going to sit here and listen to you badmouth the United States of America." —Tim Matheson as Otter in *Animal House*

Avoid the Tell

Lying experts differ on their opinions of what kind of body language will help you lie convincingly. However, they agree that it's the change in demeanor that can give you away—changes in voice, body language, and gestures. The key: keep it natural. Your target may not know what's different, but he'll notice that something's different. Study how you normally act in conversation and work on maintaining consistency. It's practice that makes a perfect liar.

"Honest ... I ran out of gas. I had a flat tire. I didn't have enough money for cab fare. My tux didn't come back from the cleaners. An old friend came in from out of town. Someone stole my car. There was an earthquake. A terrible flood. Locusts! It wasn't my fault! I swear to God!" —John Belushi as "Joliet" Jake Blues in *The Blues Brothers*

"There's a lot of things I didn't understand. There's a lot of things I'd do different if I could. Just like I think there's a lot of things you wish you could change but we can't. Some things, once they're done, can't be undone."
—Dustin Hoffman as Ted Kramer in *Kramer vs. Kramer*

———

"We all go a little mad sometimes. Haven't you?" —Anthony Perkins as Norman Bates in *Psycho*

Music

"Blame it on the night/Don't blame it on me." —Calvin Harris featuring John Newman, "Blame"

———

"Don't blame it on the sunshine/ Don't blame it on the moonlight/ Don't blame it on the good times/ Blame it on the boogie." —The Jacksons, "Blame It on the Boogie"

"Blame it on the rain . . . /Blame it on the stars . . . /Whatever you do don't put the blame on you." —Milli Vanilli, "Blame It on the Rain"

"It wasn't me, I wasn't there/I was stone drunk, it isn't clear/And it doesn't count 'cause I don't care." —Jenny Lewis and the Watson Twins, "It Wasn't Me"

"Life's a bitch and then you die, that's why we get high/'Cause you never know when you're gonna go." —Nas, "Life's a Bitch"

"Billie Jean is not my lover/She's just a girl who claims that I am the one/But the kid is not my son." — Michael Jackson, "Billie Jean"

Literature

"I would prefer not to." —Herman Melville, *Bartleby, the Scrivener*

"He always has an alibi, and one or two to spare: At whatever time the deed took place—Macavity wasn't there!" —T. S. Eliot, "Macavity: The Mystery Cat"

———•❖•———

"And the Lord God said unto the woman, what is this that thou hast done? And the woman said, the serpent beguiled me, and I did eat."—Eve's excuse about why she ate the apple, in the Bible

———•❖•———

"The Internet also makes it extraordinarily difficult for me to focus. One small break to look up exactly how almond milk is made, and four hours later I'm reading about the Donner Party and texting all my friends: DID YOU GUYS KNOW ABOUT THE DONNER PARTY AND HOW MESSED UP THAT WAS?" — Mindy Kaling, *Is Everyone Hanging Out Without Me? (And Other Concerns)*

Criminals

"Yeah, you got the family dog and the white picket fence, and you just think that's all there is. Some of us had to grow up in poverty-stricken urban neighborhoods, and we just had to adapt to our environment. I know that it's wrong. But people act like it's some crazy thing they never heard of. They don't know." —Michael Vick on his 2007 dog-fighting scandal

---

"The boys were not responsible for who they turned out to be." —Leslie Abramson, defense attorney for the Menendez brothers, who were convicted of killing their parents in 1996

"I did not, could not and would not have committed this crime." —O. J. Simpson in a statement to the judge during his 1995 murder trial

Politicos

"They're saying I groped a male staffer. Yes, I did. Not only did I grope him, I tickled him until he couldn't breathe and four guys jumped on top of me. It was my 50th birthday. It was kill the old guy. You can take anything out of context." —Former Congressman Eric Massa on behavior that led to his resignation

Political Alibis: Fake or Legit?

"I was hiking the Appalachian Trail."	Fake (Former South Carolina Governor Mark Sanford)
"I was calling my boyfriend who's on a secret foreign mission with Britain's special forces."	Fake (Saera Khan, former Norwegian parliament member)
"I'm taking five weeks off to care for endangered wombats."	Legit (Ken Henry, former Australian treasury secretary)
"It was my first time using a camera phone."	Fake (No. 9 on David Letterman's Top 10 Worst Politician Excuses)

"It depends on what the meaning of the word 'is' is." —President Bill Clinton, in a Grand Jury testimony during his 1998 impeachment trial

---

"I don't think anybody anticipated the breach of the levees. They did anticipate a serious storm." —Former President George W. Bush on the Hurricane Katrina disaster

---

"In the course of several campaigns, I started to believe that I was special and became increasingly egocentric and narcissistic." —John Edwards, after admitting to his affair, on the reason behind his error of judgment

---

"There's no question at times of my life, partially driven by how passionately I felt about this country, that I worked far too hard and things happened in my life that were not appropriate." —Newt Gingrich on his marital infidelity

"It's not elegantly stated, let me put it that way. I was speaking off the cuff in response to a question." — Mitt Romney on his remarks about the 47 percent during the 2012 presidential campaign

---

"Pictures get manipulated, pictures get dropped into accounts. We've asked an Internet security firm and a law firm to take a hard look at this to come up with a conclusion about what happened and to make sure it doesn't happen again." —Rep. Anthony Weiner denying allegations of inappropriate photos on Twitter

---

"As we know, there are known knowns; there are things we know we know. We also know there are known unknowns; that is to say we know there are some things we do not know. But there are also unknown unknowns—the ones we don't know we don't know." —Donald Rumsfeld discussing evidence of W.M.D.s in Iraq

"I meant to be 'monogamous,'
but got it mixed up with 'magnanimous.'"